WHITE COAT SECRETS

WHITE COAT SECRETS
Still Standing: A Doctor's Story

VICKIE Y. MABRY-HEIGHT, M.D., M.P.H., F.A.C.P., "COL"

Copyright © 2015 Vickie Y. Mabry-Height, M.D., M.P.H., F.A.C.P., "COL"
All rights reserved.

ISBN: 0983011710
ISBN 13: 9780983011712
Library of Congress Control Number: 2015918273
Vickie Y. Mabry-Height MD, MPH, Rancho Mirage, CA

DEDICATION

This book is dedicated to my mother, Helen Marie, whose wisdom and fortitude provided strength; to my great-grandmother, Ma Decia, who was committed to her church and God; to Wile, my great-grandfather, whose unwavering faith served as the foundation for believing in myself and my ultimate success; to the many family members, friends, and professors at York College of the City University of New York who supported me throughout this career journey; and lastly, to the ancestral spirits that paved the way for my success at a tremendous cost.

CONTENTS

Foreword xi
Author's Note xiii
Preface xv
CHAPTER 1: Just Raindrops Fight Through The Tears 1
CHAPTER 2: Cotton-Field Dreams 7
CHAPTER 3: Faith In The Face of Oppression .. 17
CHAPTER 4: Mother: "I Love You Despite Yourself" 27

CHAPTER 5:	"You Want To Be A Doctor? I don't think so."	33
CHAPTER 6:	"You Can Be Anything You Want To Be"	39
CHAPTER 7:	College—I Had To Make It!	45
CHAPTER 8:	Giving Forward	53
CHAPTER 9:	Medical School Secrets	57
CHAPTER 10:	Who Am I? Humanitarian	75
CHAPTER 11:	I Made It—The Match	87
CHAPTER 12:	Silent Tears Internship/Residency	91
CHAPTER 13:	Getting Hired—Give Me A Break	101
CHAPTER 14:	Private Practice —Navigation with No Map	111
CHAPTER 15:	The "Isms" Can't Stop Me—Racism and Sexism	123
CHAPTER 16:	Physician Entrepreneur	135
CHAPTER 17:	Master Skills for Professional Success	147

CHAPTER 18: Reflective Lessons · · · · · · · · · · · · 153

CHAPTER 19: Changing the Face of Medicine · · · 163

CHAPTER 20: Reconciliation · · · · · · · · · · · · · · · 171

About The Author · 175

FOREWORD

This book is an honest and compassionate look at the realities of a healthcare career with an emphasis on what it was like to be Black and a woman. Dr. Mabry-Height is a practicing physician in California. Despite over thirty years of education that included a doctorate in medicine, specialty training in Internal Medicine, board certification by the American Board of Internal Medicine and a Masters in Public Health, she encountered tremendous challenges trying to secure a position as a physician. She tells the story of how she became an entrepreneur to survive.

Leslie A. Lewis, Ph. D
Professor Emeritus of Biology
York College of CUNY

AUTHOR'S NOTE

The designation "COL" refers to colored physician, a stigmatizing, racial label in the *American Medical Association's (AMA) Medical Directory*, which listed all U.S. physicians. This designation resulted in discriminatory policies for more than a hundred years that were used to exclude Black physicians from medical society memberships and hospital admitting privileges. The designation is no longer used, but the legacy of discriminatory policies still exists.

Vickie Y. Mabry-Height, M.D., M.P.H., F.A.C.P., "COL"

PREFACE

This book is about how a little girl, poor and Black, born to a teenage mother out of wedlock, rose from her playground in the hot and sweaty fields of North Carolina to walk the hallowed halls of Albert Einstein College of Medicine of Yeshiva University and become a doctor.

I wanted to tell this story for other little girls, for America's fourteen million poor children, and for those with aspirations of becoming a doctor. Echoing the sentiments of my ancestors, I believe dreams are possible, but you must stand despite all obstacles, despite discouragement, and despite what some will even say are impossibilities.

I decided to become a doctor at a time when few Black Americans made it past the sixth grade, and I was the first person in my family to attend college. I survived the cotton fields of North Carolina, the ghettos of New York, as well as systemic racism and sexism in health care to achieve my dream. Because I believe there is nothing coincidental in life, many times I said to God, "Are you still listening? If you are, then tell me what all this means."

This book is part memoir, part motivational message, and part mandate for change in the field of medicine. This is my experience as a Black, American, female physician, in my words and in my voice. I'm pulling back the covers to reveal the pain and perseverance

PREFACE

in my journey in hopes of preparing others who may face similar obstacles and challenges. There are also career and life lessons here for anyone seeking personal and professional advancement. The world of work has changed. A good education is no guarantee of a good job. Despite an excellent education, I had to become an entrepreneur.

Finally, I'll highlight and offer thoughts on changes desperately needed in the health-care industry. Lack of diversity, inequality, and the health disparity gap have all reached critical points. Did you know that the percentage of Black physicians in the United States in 1950 was more than it is today? In 1950 2.3% of American physicians were Black. Fifty-three years later in 2003 it was 2.6%, and in 2007, according to the Sullivan Report it was 2.0%. Did you know that Black Americans are more likely to die of preventable medical conditions? These are astonishing facts when you consider the advancements made through civil rights and increased access to education and health care. This goes beyond politics and economics—these are matters of life and death.

As I was writing this book, I could hear an echo of the lyrics of "Don't Let Me Be Misunderstood," sung by Nina Simone. I hope my message will not be misunderstood as you read this book. Although I have overcome incredible odds to succeed in medicine, drawing from my life experiences as well as lessons learned, I offer these insights to motivate and inspire your success. I hope you find this book useful and thought-provoking.

CHAPTER 1

JUST RAINDROPS
FIGHT THROUGH THE TEARS

Speak up! What you have to say matters. Do not suffer in silence.

It was about one o'clock in the afternoon and I was on a Trailways bus arriving in Ayden, North Carolina. Each year when school in New York ended, my mother would put me on a bus headed south, so I could spend the summer with my great-grandparents.

As the bus pulled into the gas station, I could see my great-grandmother, Ma Decia, standing near the sidewalk, awaiting my arrival. She was staring at the bus as it pulled in, searching each window. It was an unusually cold and windy day. Just as I stepped off the bus, it began to rain. It rained harder and harder until the raindrops were so large that we felt as if we were being beaten. But I can still remember the feeling of warmth from my great-grandmother's body as she held me close, trying to shelter me from the rain.

We were waiting for my great-grandfather to come and pick us up in his car. It was raining so hard that my great-grandmother's clothing was drenched and she began to shiver. She went inside the gas station and asked the white owner if we could come out of the rain for a few minutes.

He snarled like an angry animal and then shouted "Get the hell out of my store!" She did not respond. She politely backed out of the store and into the cold downpour with me at her side. As I looked up at her warm, brown face and drenched, gray hair, I could see that she was crying. This was the first time I had ever seen my great-grandmother cry. I held her closer because I was also crying and hoped the rain would conceal my tears. What I could not express to her at the time was the emotional pain and humiliation that I felt deep in my soul as I witnessed her being treated in such a demeaning manner and talked to as if she were not even human. But my great-grandmother was intuitive, and when she saw me crying, she whispered in her usual soft, melodic voice, "Don't let this upset you. A little water won't hurt us."

It was the great Louis Armstrong who said that he could never go back to Georgia again because each time he tried, it brought back all of the bad feelings and emotions he had endured while living there as a child. After this, I understood what he meant. Even now, years later, whenever I tell this story, I am sad and a part of me weeps inside.

In hindsight, I realize that my great-grandmother was trying to protect me from the oppression that they had endured as a regular part of their daily lives. She did not want to me grow up with hatred for anyone, and she wanted me to have a better life.

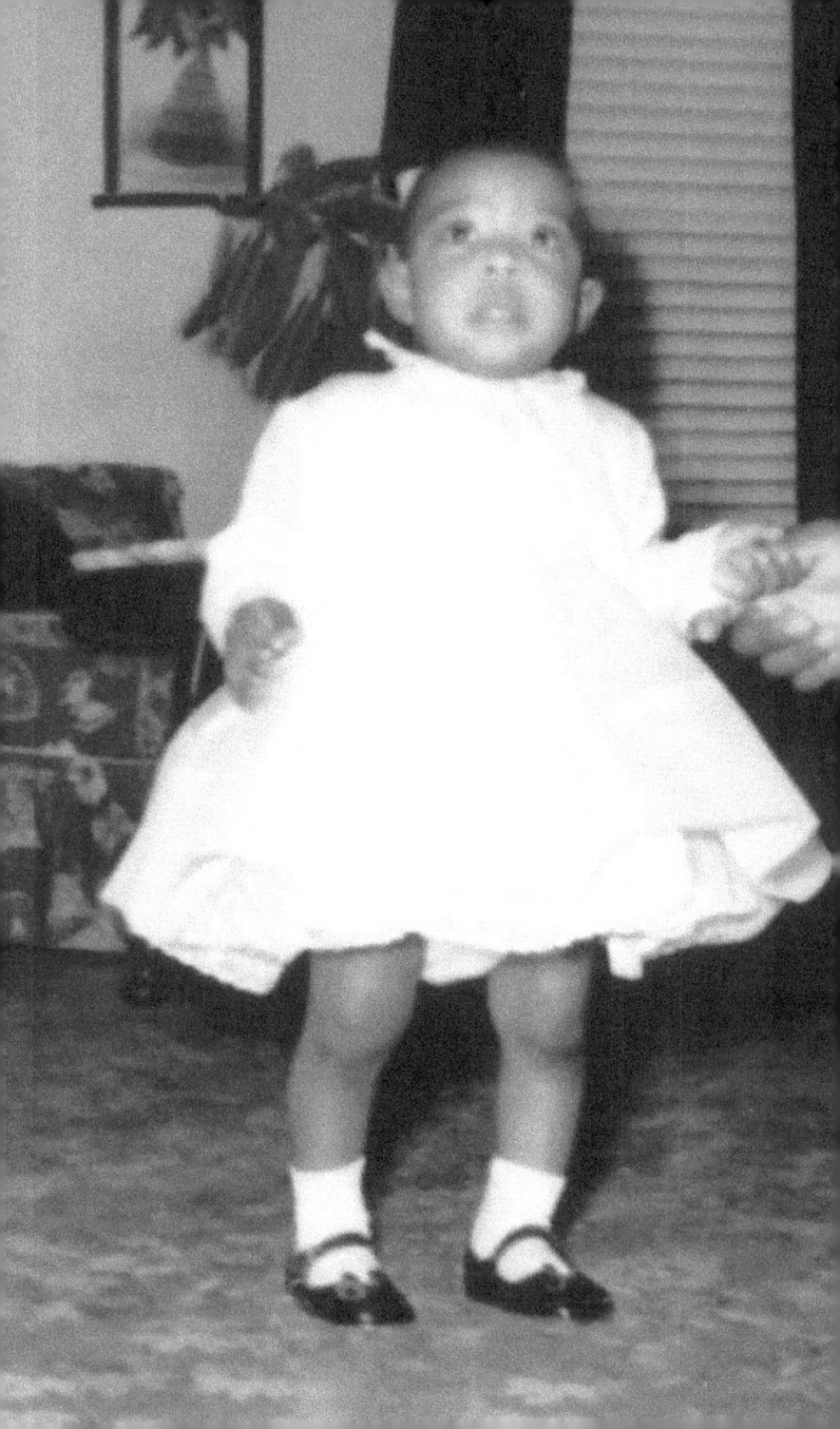

CHAPTER 2

COTTON-FIELD DREAMS

Give your children permission to dream. You never know where those dreams may lead.

The cotton fields of North Carolina were my playground. I played alongside my great-grandfather, whom I called Grandpa. He made a small, cotton sack especially for me that draped across one of my shoulders, and he would leave every third or fourth cotton plant for me to pick. I could not have been happier as I followed behind him as he picked row after row of cotton. I would try to mimic him and as a child it was all play. The only thing I hated was, every now and then, I would encounter a "bow weevil" worm on a cotton plant. These were frightening, and I would not pick those pieces of cotton.

Grandpa worked from sunup to sundown in those fields, earning a meager wage. He always wore blue jean overalls over a long-sleeved shirt. His skin was a golden-copper color, and he had light-brown eyes and a smile that always made me smile. His voice was deep, and he wore a cap that was tilted to the side of his bald head. I can still hear the echo of his soft baritone voice encouraging me to pursue my dreams so I would not have to work in the fields. At the end of each week, I would receive a white envelope from Grandpa with two dollars as pay for all the hours I had worked.

As a young man, Grandpa worked as a carpenter for a construction company. One day, he fell from the roof and injured his right shoulder and his right arm swung in the wind because of that injury. There was no worker's compensation in those days, and he was let go from his job. But Grandpa was a survivor, and he was able to work at various odd jobs, including in the cotton and tobacco fields.

At the crack of dawn, even before the rooster crowed, Grandpa was awake and getting dressed to head to the fields. This was his everyday routine. My great-grandmother would be up cooking breakfast, and you could smell the food cooking all over the house.

No child who wasn't Black, poor, and southern could have understood what it meant to be born in the South in the early 1950s. In North Carolina, I quickly learned my place because it was similar to Mississippi and what Dr. Martin Luther King Jr. called "sweltering with the heat of injustice and oppression."

Our trips into town to the grocery store made it clear what was expected of Black people. I wondered why my great-grandfather would step off the sidewalk and look down to avoid eye contact whenever a white person approached him. I dared not drink from the water fountains labeled "Whites Only." I mimicked his behavior because I thought it was normal and did not know it was a symptom of the venom we endured regularly.

Grandpa wanted more for me. Racial matters were never discussed in my presence. My great-grandparents' message always focused elsewhere, with nothing to detract from hope and endless possibilities. They wanted me to know that I could be anything I wanted to be, and they sheltered me from the storm.

Grandpa would tell me stories about his grandfather, who he said was brought to America shackled in chains as a slave. My great-grandparents would have been happy to read North Carolina's "Sorry for Slavery" apology that was published on April 06, 2007. Natural consequences of living under constant terrorism are fear, anxiety, depression, and so on, leading to adverse health effects such as hypertension, chronic depression, adverse outcomes, and death at an early age.

I asked my great-grandpa one day how he survived during the Depression, and he said it was not so bad. They had always grown their own fruits and vegetables, and on the farm, they raised their own animals, so mostly, they only bought sugar, flour, and sometimes "store-bought bread." Anyway, he said he preferred grandma's hot, buttered biscuits rather than store-bought bread. Thinking back, I guess what he was really saying was they had had nothing for so long that they did not miss the things they had never had.

He told me stories about his childhood and how he had to walk miles to school while the school buses drove past him with the white kids. I did not know at the time that it would be these ancestral stories that would help me persevere during the rough times.

Growing up poor and Black in America taught me that I wasn't worth anything. I wasn't valued, and despite the Civil Rights Act, Black Americans still had to endure daily indignities. Nevertheless, I was fortunate because my great-grandparents, my church, my friends, and one schoolteacher said I could be anything I dreamed I could be.

My great-grandparents had sixth-grade educations because that was the highest grade offered to Black

Americans in the South in the early 1950s. They could not attend school the entire year because they had to work in the fields, harvesting tobacco, cotton, and anything else that grew in the South. They always felt that they would not have been poor if they had been able to obtain a better education.

Education symbolized freedom. They taught me that education was my way out. "Get a good education," they told me. "No one can take that away from you." They also believed that I would get a better education if I lived in the North. It was because of this that I did not continue living with my great-grandparents and eventually moved North. Their encouragement helped foster in me an eagerness to learn. I decided very early in life to get the best education possible. I followed my great-grandparents around, listening to every word they said about how to succeed. Because the importance of an education was drilled into me at such an early age, I never missed a day of school and always completed my homework assignments. I was determined to earn my freedom.

Looking back, I now realize that my great-grandparents were my first mentors. They believed in me, so I believed in myself. They sheltered me from much of the racist and terrorist environment that surrounded us.

Parents, grandparents, and teachers can make a big difference in the lives of children. Their words can awaken purpose and instill confidence or crush dreams. Have you ever noticed how some parents and grandparents speak about their children? They say, "This one is the doctor. That one is the lawyer." They speak possibility and purpose into their children from a very early age. I'm not suggesting that you pick and pronounce your child's career at age four. But what you say to and about children has a greater impact than most would imagine.

It's also important to challenge your children to work hard at an early age. I don't advocate the "tiger mom" approach, but you would be amazed at what your children can accomplish with appropriate encouragement and support.

CHAPTER 3

FAITH IN THE FACE OF OPPRESSION

*There are good and bad
folks in all churches and nationalities.*

I lived with my great-grandparents, Will and Ma Decia, on the farm in Ayden, North Carolina, until I was age five. Grandpa was my great-grandmother's second husband. They never had any children together, but he took care of the entire family and all of the children as if they were his own.

On the farm, there were chickens, pigs, and cows. We grew potatoes, corn, cabbage, collard greens, sweet potatoes, and watermelons. My job every morning was to collect the eggs. Sometimes I broke a few eggs while playing with the baby chicks. I loved those early years and summers on the farm because my great-grandfather never talked to me as if I were a child. He always spoke to me about his life and the things he had learned.

The nearest grocery store was a ten-mile walk into town. The trip took several hours each way. When my great-grandfather allowed me to go along, it was exciting for me because I'd help carry some of the grocery bags and he would talk to me about life. I can still remember him telling me that if I wanted to be successful, I should "find a need and fill it." It was only in hindsight that I realized my great-grandfather's trips to the grocery store must have been filled with deep fears and trepidation, things no one should have to experience just doing grocery shopping. Grandpa also taught me about relationships with people. He would say, "Help a friend to success, and then that person will help you."

My great-grandparents were very religious and attended church nearly every evening and all day on Sunday. We spent all of Saturday cooking and preparing for church the next day. Grandma always had a special hat for church on Sunday, and I remember how glamorous she looked when she put on her Sunday hat. Church was not just about religion; it was about community. It was a time to come together, receive encouragement, and share life stories. We attended Pleasant Plains Church in Ayden, North Carolina. At one time, my great-grandparents did not have a car and the deacon of the church, Buddy Jackson, was kind enough to pick us up every Sunday morning to make sure we got there on time.

A dilemma for me was how members of the Ku Klux Klan also attended church on Sunday and then lynched Black folk all over the South the other six days of the week. When I asked Grandma about this she said, "There are good and bad folk in all churches and nationalities." In our home, they never taught hatred for anyone, but Grandpa always slept with a shotgun leaning against the wall near his bed.

Because my great-grandfather had a heart condition, the local doctor frequently visited our home. He was an older Black gentleman who always dressed well and carried one of those old-fashioned medicine bags like you see in the movies. My great-grandfather always seemed to feel better after each visit. I remember thinking that if I were a doctor, I could help people feel better, too. I asked the doctor lots of questions, including whether he thought I could become a doctor when I grew up. "You can certainly become a nurse," he said. I can still see the smile and reassuring look on his face. "Study hard, do well in school, and you will make a fine nurse."

This wouldn't be the last time someone would try to put my head on straight or set my sights in a more realistic direction. Thankfully, I was a stubborn child, and my great-grandparents were there to nurture my dreams. They told me, "You are smart. You can be anything you want to be as long as you get a good education." That was the message they drilled into me over and over. But that early experience with the doctor was the spark that started me on my journey to becoming a physician.

It was not easy. There were times when I doubted whether I would make it, but there would always be that proverbial ram in the bush to remind me of my great-grandparents' words. I've learned that impossible dreams are God's version of the future. They wait for someone who dares to believe and take action.

Someone will always have an opinion about your dreams. Most of these people are well-meaning, but their opinions are rarely based on your true potential. Often, opinions are limited by convention, culture, perception, and people's beliefs about what is or isn't possible for themselves. They think they are doing you a favor by letting you down easily or protecting you from the harsh world.

There's a scene in the movie *The Pursuit of Happiness* when Chris Gardner (Will Smith) is playing basketball with his son. Gardner tells his son that he was a below-average basketball player. "You'll probably be about as good as I was," he says. "That's kind of the way it works. I was below average, so you'll probably ultimately rank somewhere around there." He tells his son, "You'll excel at a lot of things, just not this. I don't want you out here shooting this ball around all day and night." His son throws the ball down and walks away. Like my great-grandparents, in that moment Gardner has the awareness and wisdom to touch the heart of his son. His son didn't necessarily have hoop dreams, but he did need permission to dream. "Don't ever let somebody tell you, you can't do something. Not even me," Gardner says firmly. "You got a dream, you got to protect it. When people can't do something themselves, they want to tell you that you can't do it. You want something, go get it. Period."

All achievement springs from the courage to dream. It's not whether the dream is realistic; the important thing to nurture in ourselves and others is the courage to dream impossible dreams. Listen to the dreams of those around you. Then, help their dreams live. Speak words that awaken hope. Offer love, wisdom, and a helping hand. Give their dreaming hearts permission and even the fuel to soar. You never know where those dreams may lead.

CHAPTER 4

MOTHER: "I LOVE YOU DESPITE YOURSELF"

Prioritize your family. You cannot get the time you missed with them back.

My mother's name was Helen Marie, and her favorite saying was, "I love you despite yourself." She had not yet finished high school when she became pregnant with me. She had been dating another high school student in a nearby town and telephoned his home when she found out she was pregnant. His brother, Theodore, answered and told her that my father had joined the military. She asked Theodore to tell my father that she was pregnant. But Theodore didn't tell my father until years later that he had a daughter.

There were tremendous financial and emotional costs to my mother as a single, teenage parent. Somehow I think I became her hope. I often thank God she did not abort me. Although the major causes of death in Black Americans include heart disease, cancer, strokes, diabetes, unintentional injuries, and homicides, the leading cause of death every year that exceeds all of the top ten causes combined for Black Americans is abortion.

MOTHER: "I LOVE YOU DESPITE YOURSELF"

I met my father for the first time when I was twenty-seven. He was tall, light-skinned, and soft-spoken. His hair was curly, and he seemed like a nice person, but to me, he was a stranger. My mother said that she had decided to tell me about him because if she died, I would never have known my real father. I didn't consider him my father though; the father I knew was my great-grandfather, who had raised me from childhood. We did not discuss having any future meetings, and I never developed a relationship with my father. As far as I was concerned, my mom was both mother and father, so to me she was a mother-father. Also, after my great-grandfather died, I celebrated each Father's Day by sending gifts to my mother.

In 1990, my mother died from cancer. It was at this time that I had to navigate the murky waters of health care. I received a telephone call—my mother was dying from cancer and was expected to live less than six months. I desperately searched for a hospice facility but was told, "We have a two-year waiting list." Bewildered, I remembered my great-grandmother always said, "God works in mysterious ways." The administrator of the hospice affiliated with the medical school I had attended sounded hesitant as he said, "I will get back to you." Days felt like months, but three days later, he called. "We have a bed for her." There were tears of joy—I called her every day. Sometimes, I could feel her pain as I heard her grimacing as she said, hello in her uniquely soft, melodic voice. I whispered, "Mom, how are you feeling today?"

One day, she said, "Oh, terrific." As a physician, I knew that meant morphine, her pain medication, had been increased. Hurting and helpless, I shivered as sadness rippled through my body, and I held back tears. With the thought the cancer is spreading, warm tears streamed down both cheeks, leaving tracks in my make-up. As it became obvious that she was nearing her demise—a river of tears wet all of the papers on my desk. As I began to think I might never see her alive again, I fell into an ugly cry until there was a knock on the door and a voice said, "Doctor, your next patient is waiting."

In retrospect, I would advise anyone with a family to get help and to not feel guilty about not being able to do everything for your family. However, do not neglect important things because time is the one thing you can never get back. Always remember, there are things that your family needs that they can only get from you.

CHAPTER 5

"YOU WANT TO BE A DOCTOR? I DON'T THINK SO."

Words can awaken purpose and instill confidence, or crush dreams.

I was five years old when my mother took me to New York City to live with her. We lived in Brooklyn with my aunt and uncle. The apartment was on the second floor of an old brownstone and I shared a room with my cousin.

I was happy to be with my mother, but it was a long way from the farm. I missed my great-grandparents and the farm animals. Happily though, every year that I lived in New York, I summered in North Carolina with my great-grandparents. It was a long ride on the Trailways bus. I always traveled in the front seat, across from the driver, who would not let me off the bus until my great-grandmother met me at the stop. My mother packed a sack lunch for me: a fried-chicken sandwich and a slice of vanilla cake with chocolate icing.

My mother later moved us to our own apartment in the Bedford–Stuyvesant area of Brooklyn. Initially, she worked as a seamstress at a local factory. She loved to sew and often made her own clothing, bedspreads, draperies, and matching dresses for us. Later, she passed the GED test and then trained as a nurse's aide at night. This resulted in several positions where she worked as a private care taker for disabled persons in their home. Sometimes, she would let me go to work with her for a day, so I could see firsthand what she was doing. I still remember one of her patients who had Parkinson's disease. Although I did not understand all the symptoms associated with this condition, when I was in medical school and we studied this disease, it was this early experience with my mom that really helped me understand it.

In public school, my first-grade teacher was Mrs. Enen. She was a petite, Italian woman with jet-black hair cut into a bob hairstyle. I loved school and could not wait to get home to do my homework. My mother often helped me with my homework in the evening, after she got home. Because it was time that we spent together, it encouraged me to do well in school. I valued the attention she gave me even though she was exhausted.

It was a middle-school science teacher, a middle-aged Caucasian man, who first made me conscious of racism. I had told him that I dreamed of becoming a doctor when I grew up. One day in class, he handed me my paper with a big, red C written on it and said, "You want to be a doctor? I don't think so." His negative comment might have crushed my dreams of ever becoming a physician, but my great-grandfather had done his job well. I made sure to never again share my aspirations with teachers. There were times when I didn't think I was smart enough to become a doctor, but my great-grandfathers' voice was always there.

Children need affirmation and support. There will always be people out there waiting to tell them what they can't do. Our job is to make sure our voices are there, filling their hearts with courage and confidence.

CHAPTER 6

"YOU CAN BE ANYTHING YOU WANT TO BE"

*Children need permission to dream
and the confidence topursue their
dreams despite the opinions of others.*

I had decided that I was definitely going to enter medicine as a career by the time I reached my last year of high school. The trouble was, no one ever told me about college admission requirements or what was required to enter medical school.

My mother and I started looking at colleges I could attend, investigating costs, and talking about how I would pay for a medical school education. I met with my high-school guidance counselor to find out more about colleges but never received the information I requested. Instead, she encouraged me to forget about college—at least for a few years—and said, "Get a job, and help your poor family."

You must be able to fight obstacles like this. As a child, I did not recognize this as an obstacle and thought it was good advice that I should truly consider, until I relayed it to my mother. That evening, in the course of our conversation at the dinner table, my mother said something that I will never forget: "You probably have another forty or fifty years to work. I think you need to go to college and get an education, so you can pursue your dream of becoming a physician." These words helped keep me going through all the discouragement.

When things were hard and I wanted to quit, I would always come back to those words and think, if I quit because it's hard now, I'm going to have forty or fifty years to regret not being able to do what I wanted to do.

My mother was very protective of me. She knew what the ghetto could do to children and their aspirations. I could not hang out after school like my friends. She even went so far as to select my friends by telling me who to stay away from. When I became a teenager, I tried to explain that she couldn't pick my friends my entire life. Still, she demanded that I not associate with certain people. Eventually, I learned that she was right. One day, while I was walking to school, I noticed a boy I knew standing in a doorway. He appeared lethargic. He was barely able to stand up and even seemed to be drooling, which made me think he was high on drugs.

Now that I am older, I realize he was most likely addicted to heroin. It was moments like this that made me acutely aware of why my mother was so protective of me. The impediments to my dreams weren't always on the streets. Most of my counselors and teachers never expected me to finish high school or succeed at anything.

To students and parents with children who are aspiring to be doctors, I would advise that you:

- Make sure you are able to overcome obstacles like the counselors advice I referenced above.

- Take advanced classes in high school, so your GPA will be higher than 4.0.
- Do not wait until medical school to take anatomy. Take it in high school if possible.
- Take public speaking as early as possible. It is never too early to develop confidence in verbalizing your thoughts to others.
- Enroll in a pipeline program that has demonstrated successful outcomes in preparing students for medical careers. An example is "Profiles for Success," a six-week course at the University of Michigan.
- Take advanced biochemistry in college to help prepare you for medical school.
- Do *not* take the Medical College Admission Test (MCAT) without completing a preparatory course because you will be guaranteed a low score.

CHAPTER 7

COLLEGE—I HAD TO MAKE IT!

Seek out mentors early. No one succeeds alone.

I graduated from John Dewey High School in three years and then enrolled at York College of the City University of New York in Jamaica, Queens. Overall, college was a wonderful experience. It was just seven miles from my home, so I often walked to school. But the hardest part about college for me was living at home. The evening hours were noisy, with everyone discussing the events of their day. I spent lots of time in the library. I learned to go to bed early and wake up around midnight to work when the house was quiet. It was challenging, but the support of my family made a big difference. I didn't have to worry about rent, food or clothing. There was also no tuition to pay because at that time the City University of New York had a special program for students with low incomes. I had to do work study in the college library while I was in college to earn money that covered my books and materials.

In addition, I worked part-time at a local fast-food restaurant during my first year of college. It was not too long before I noticed a drop in my test scores. My mother insisted that I quit the job and concentrate full-time on my studies. It made a tremendous difference in my grades.

The best part of college was the faculty. The class sizes were small, so I could develop relationships with the instructors. There were so many kind and generous professors at York College. Most of my professors seemed genuinely interested in me as a person and encouraged me to pursue becoming a doctor. During my senior year, one of the professors asked me to assist him on a biochemistry research project, which I did. I learned a lot working with him, and having my name on a published paper certainly helped my chances of getting into medical school. That same instructor was also kind enough to write a letter of recommendation for me.

It was my genetics instructor who really mentored me. He took the time to talk to me not just about school but about life in general. One day after class, in his office, he told me, as you become more and more successful, you have to "learn to measure your success by your enemies. Because the higher you climb the ladder of success, the more of them you will have." It's been more than thirty years since I finished college, but I am still in touch with my genetics professor. He wrote a character reference that helped me qualify for the health-care-leadership fellowship I started in 2002. No one succeeds alone. It is important who you know, what you know, and who knows you.

It's important to seek out mentors and be open to mentorship throughout your life. The benefit is not just the formal instruction and practical help you can receive, but also the informal wisdom and understanding you gain through conversations with them over the course of your relationship. Not everyone will want to mentor or help you. Some may even go out of their way to discourage or delay your progress. But don't let a few negative people keep you from the benefits that can come to you.

Avoid toxic people at all costs.

Remember, in order to find the right people in life, you have to be willing to weather some wrong people, which includes family members and colleagues. I must admit that I have not had the best relationship with my siblings and things did not always work out well with other family members either. Nevertheless, I still love them, and one of the things I have learned is that most families are dysfunctional and all that changes in families are the names. Avoid all toxic people whenever you encounter them, no matter what your relationship to them might be. The subject of challenging relationships within families is another book that I have yet to write.

Every dream requires a team.

The support I received from my family encouraged me to stretch myself in school. I took on a relatively heavy course load throughout college. I completed the required courses for an undergraduate degree in three years and spent my senior year taking advanced biochemistry and genetics in preparation for medical school.

My family was proud when I graduated at the top of my class from the City University of New York. The day was filled with excitement; my mother and my sisters and brothers attended my graduation ceremony. I felt a sense of accomplishment and did not realize at the time that it was the beginning of a very long and painful career in health care.

I didn't have time for much of a social life in college except one very special friend. She was not a science major but took several science courses. She was an extremely hardworking student. In fact, she was our class valedictorian. Because we were lab partners, we spent most afternoons completing laboratory work in genetics. We are still friends to this day, and she visits me when she travels to California.

CHAPTER 8

GIVING FORWARD

Don't forget to volunteer. You can only get so far working for money.

Volunteering at a local Catholic hospital had a lasting impact on me. I assisted with children who had been born with various birth defects and neurological syndromes.

These were children not normally seen in our communities because they are often institutionalized early in life. For example, one of the children had Treacher Collins Syndrome, which resulted in her eyes being located on the side of her head, like a fish, and she was deaf from deformed ears. She would turn her head to the side to look at me, and she smiled whenever I held her. This certainly made me appreciate how fortunate families with healthy children are.

Most memorable was a young, white boy who had no arms and no legs. His mother had been treated with thalidomide during her pregnancy, and this was a side effect of that treatment. He loved being hugged, something he could not reciprocate. It really taught me to appreciate the small things, like hugs, that so many of us take for granted. It was my experiences with children like this that helped reaffirm my decision to enter medicine. Initially, I wanted to be a pediatrician so I could help children like this.

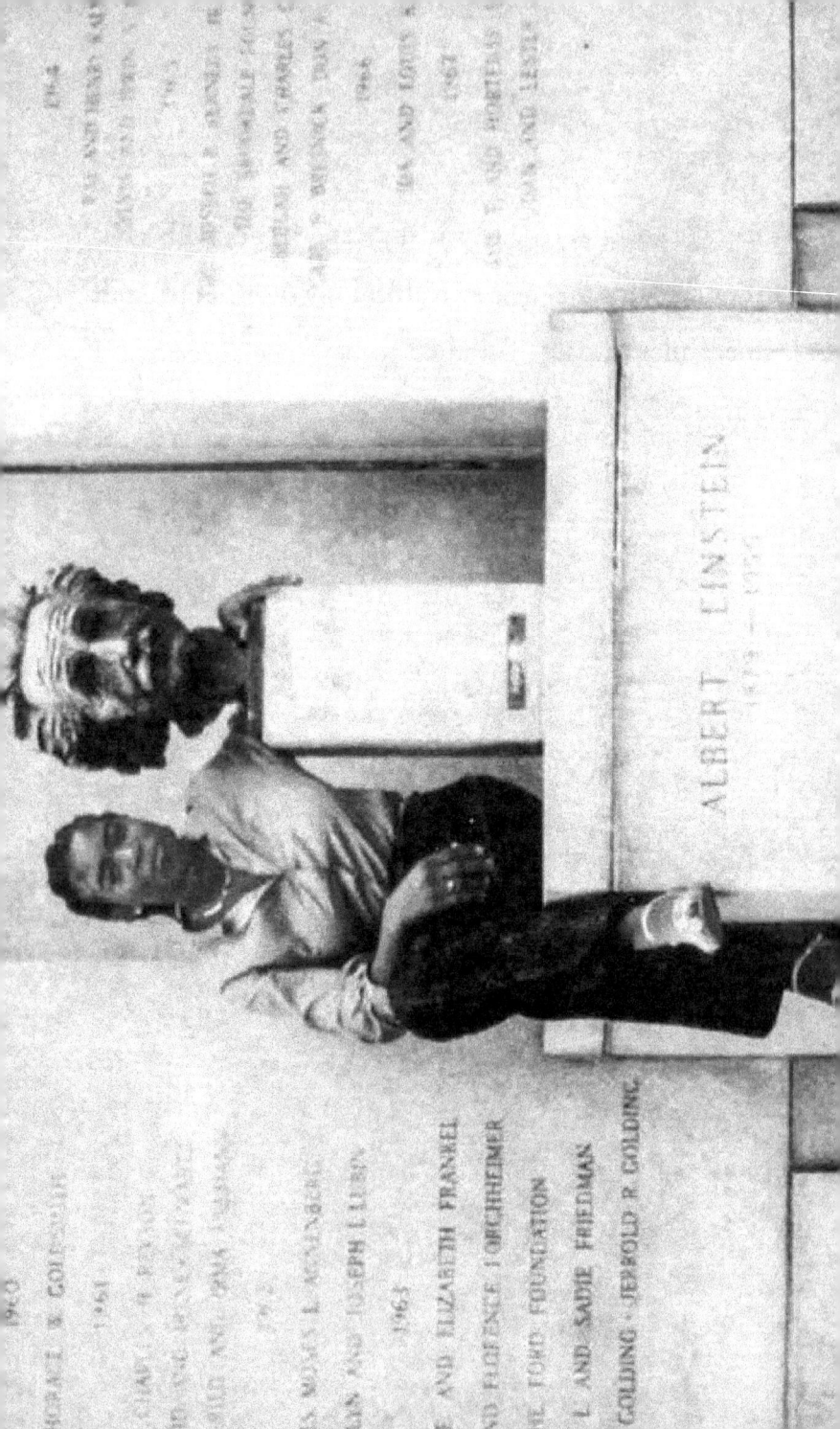

CHAPTER 9

MEDICAL SCHOOL SECRETS

Sometimes your best is not good enough. Do whatever it takes to accomplish your goal.

I finished college with a nearly 4.0 GPA, and I did well on the MCAT, which is required to enter medical school. When it was time to apply to medical school, I was fairly optimistic that I would get accepted somewhere. I applied to a total of ten schools, including some state universities and six of them top medical schools at the time. I received letters of acceptance from six schools. It was one of my college professors that helped me select Albert Einstein College of Medicine of Yeshiva University in the Bronx, New York, as my first choice.

I was so excited when I received a letter stating that I would receive a full scholarship at the Albert Einstein College of Medicine. It was one of the top ten medical schools in the country at that time. A full scholarship is very hard to walk away from when you're from a poor family. There were a total of 126 students in my medical school class. Nine of them were minority students. The minority students included four students who were Black descendants of slaves: three women and one man.

I still remember my first day at Einstein. I was lighthearted because I was receiving a full scholarship, which I believed would allow me to complete my medical education without incurring thousands of dollars of student loan debt. What I did not know at the time was that "full scholarship" is a misnomer. Before I arrived, the financial-aid counselor had already calculated all my expenses and handed me a letter explaining the full scholarship. Basically, it was a check for $2,500 that I would receive each year for the first two years. I would receive nothing in the last two years. My counselor then outlined several loans I would have to apply for to cover the balance of the tuition as well as books, housing, and other expenses. So the scholarship did not cover the bulk of my costs, not even the full tuition for the first two years.

When I graduated, I owed over $300,000 in student loans. The expense was magnified because interest on the loan principal had accumulated from the day I had signed the documents. In other words, the payments had been deferred but not the interest, which had accrued over my four years of school. Furthermore, the intensity of the classes in medical school made it impossible for me to work to pay back any debt while I was still attending.

I encourage young people to speak to the financial-aid officers of any school they are seriously considering. Ask them to be very clear about whether you are eligible for scholarships and, if so, what they will cover. I'm not sure I would have gone into medicine had I known I would incur such a phenomenal debt. I certainly would have considered and researched other, less costly career choices.

I did not know that after graduation from medical school, I would spend the next twenty years of my life paying substantial monthly sums.

Still, my mother told me not to worry about money because I would be able to pay it back. She was of the opinion that there are no unemployed doctors. She was right; I was eventually able to pay all of my education loans, but it took many years.

I learned later that if I had attended one of the historically black medical schools, I might have received more financial assistance due to need. The grants and scholarships available at those schools are not available at all medical schools. I now believe that grants and scholarships based upon financial need should follow the student no matter which school he or she chooses to attend.

Medical school was an extremely lonely time for me. I missed being with my family and seeing my mother every day. I missed her daily words of encouragement, which had nourished my soul. Albert Einstein's student body was largely Jewish, and as a Black American who was not Jewish, I did not feel as if I belonged. The alienation I felt made the environment difficult for me. It was a challenging experience, and it helped me be cognizant of other cultures and religious beliefs. I never socialized with any other students at Einstein, and I never ate in the school cafeteria. Sometimes I studied with a friend who was from Haiti, but even that was rare.

During my first year, I continued to live at home and commuted each day to save money, but this caused me to lose many hours of valuable study time. The second year, I moved onto campus.

The work pace was phenomenal. I had very little time for family, friends, myself, or any of the things I had once enjoyed. For example, the entire year of biochemistry I had taken in college was covered in about three months; if I had not taken advanced biochemistry in college, I would not have been able to pass it in medical school. Fortunately, my professors at York College had prepared me well. If you plan to attend medical school, take biochemistry in college if possible.

The classes at Albert Einstein College of Medicine were from Monday through Friday, all day, but I rarely attended class because I felt so ostracized by the Jewish students. I only attended class if I felt I had to in order to better understand a particular concept and/or attendance was mandatory. So much of what I learned was self-taught from textbooks and syllabi. Sometimes I would study the syllabus and textbook and only go to class to take the final test. I passed most of my classes this way.

The school was very supportive in providing tutors when you asked for help. I studied twelve hours a day, including weekends. I had never considered myself smart, so I just worked hard, reading until I understood the material. There was a lot of self-teaching. It was almost impossible to get answers out of instructors. I remember asking a question in a pathology laboratory and being told by the instructor to find the answer myself, so I did.

Anatomy was more challenging because I'd had very little of it in college. I think it's great that some high schools teach anatomy today. Such early exposure certainly would have helped me! Anatomy was so difficult that among students, it was known as the course that separated the men from the boys. Medical students who could not pass anatomy often did not graduate. What helped me get through it was the help of another minority student who was a couple of years ahead of me. He would test me after I studied and answer my questions. He also encouraged me to make flash cards because there were so many things that we had to commit to memory. I still get butterflies in my stomach when I remember looking down the long hallway at the list of names of who had passed the class. I was elated when I saw the *P* for passed next to my social security number.

I took the summer off after completing my first year of medical school. We were told to enjoy ourselves because it would be the last summer vacation until we graduated three years later. I spent time with my family and worked to save some money.

Don't let being poor stop you from having dreams and going after them.

The next three years consisted of month after month of continuous, intensive study. The classes were tough, and the isolation made it extremely stressful. At the time, I thought they were the worst four years of my life. There were many days that I wanted to give up because the work was just too hard and I didn't feel I could do it. That was when I would call my mother. She would tell me that if I wanted to clean people's houses, no one would bother me or question anything I said or did, but if I should decide to do anything other than that, I would be challenged. In fact, just that alone told me it was worth doing. She would say, "Just hang in there, and keep going."

My mother and great-grandparents encouraged me to keep going. They constantly reinforced that I could do it. Mom said, "If other people are doing it, it's humanly possible. You are human, so you can do it too." Sometimes I would telephone my aunt Sis, who was a minister in North Carolina, and she would say a prayer for me over the telephone. If it had not been for the constant support and words of encouragement from my family, I would never have survived medical school.

Have you ever had a miracle happen to you?

Medical school also included practical experience with patients. These rotations were called "clerkships." My first clerkship was a rotation in adult internal medicine, and the first patient assigned to me had rheumatoid arthritis. This patient's history was the first I had to obtain, and he was the first patient I ever had to examine.

Following getting the history and the examination, I had to present the case to the attending physician the next morning at what was called "attending rounds." I was stressed because I had never done this before. I remembered a black woman who was a couple of years ahead of me named Beverly. She had told me that if I ever needed help, I could call her. I was hesitant because sometimes people say that, but they don't really mean it. Nevertheless, I telephoned her at about six o'clock in the evening, and she came and helped me obtain the patients' history, examine him, and organize my presentation for the next morning. We discussed differential diagnoses, treatment, the examination's findings, and so on. I was well prepared the next morning and presented the case with no problems. The attending was impressed, and I will always be grateful to Beverly for helping me.

The clerkships covered various specialties in medicine, and some of them included working with an intern who was caring for patients in the hospital.

I considered myself lucky because I had been assigned to work with the upperclassman who had helped me with anatomy. He was truly a mentor, recognized my hard work, and genuinely wanted me to do well.

I remember caring for one of his patients, a thirty-three-year-old woman who was dying of leukemia. I can still recall standing at her bedside when she took her last breath. It was the first time I witnessed someone's death. I immediately called for one of the nurses, who closed the patient's eyes and pulled the bed sheet up to her neck, so she looked peaceful.

Medical school never taught me how to tell a family their loved one had died.

Because the intern was so busy, the nurse and I had to tell the patients' nine children that their mother had died. I felt so nervous walking into that room, where people were crying and screaming. I was fortunate that the nurse was there to support me. The family asked to see their mother, so we accompanied them to the room, where they spent some time alone with her.

Once they left, I found the intern to tell him about the experience. I could immediately see the anger on his face. He was disappointed and had been wondering where I was for several hours. There was a visible change in his demeanor once I told him what had happened.

I worked so hard that, when my clerkship ended, I felt disappointed I had not received honors as part of my evaluation. I asked my intern about this, and he said, "You didn't want honors. If you knew what the girl that got honors had to do, believe me, you would not want it." I did not understand what he meant, and he never elaborated or explained. This was one of those things that no one talked about. Only one student in each clerkship rotation receives honors. What was explained to me later was that some students work very hard, while others take the easy way out and sleep their way to honors by having sex with the attending.

Success is being able to support yourself doing what you love.

It's important to make decisions about what you will and won't do to succeed. Your reputation and integrity are important. Stick to your standards. It may make things more difficult for you. You may miss out on opportunities and promotions in the short run, but holding on to your integrity will pay off. It is important to realize that integrity is not for sale.

I learned a lot during the clerkship rotations. All of them were intimidating, and often, they were humiliating encounters. If I asked questions, they were not answered, and frequently, I was told to find answers on my own. Once, I responded to a situation indicating that I had done my best and was told by one of the teaching doctors, "Sometimes your best is not good enough. You have to learn to do whatever it takes to get the job done." It was encounters like this that I would remember for the rest of my life.

There were many racial slurs. I remember one day, there was an abnormal x-ray, and the instructor commented that there must have been a "nigger in the pile" of x-rays. One day in class, an instructor made a racist remark that made me angry. When I got home, I wrote a response that I submitted to the school newspaper. I was told that if it had been published, there would have been repercussions that included my not being able to graduate, so I withdrew the response.

The ancestral spirits stood behind me.

Racism still exists, in medicine and in almost every profession. I had to learn to treat myself well during these times. I would call my family members to hear words of encouragement. I often had to remind myself that "This too shall pass." Thoughts of what my ancestors had endured during slavery also gave me encouragement. Sometimes, it was as if the ancestral spirits were standing behind me; compared to the brutality and terrorism that they endured, whatever I was going through was trivial. I finally finished all the clerkship rotations.

CHAPTER 10

WHO AM I? HUMANITARIAN

*Success is not about how you look.
It is about how you see yourself."*

The clerkships were followed by elective courses in the last year of medical school. I selected an elective in community health. One day, I saw a brochure on a bulletin board from the National Medical Fellowship indicating that they provided research grants. Around the same time, I read an article about hundreds of children and babies dying in East Africa from central-nervous-system tuberculosis. Why were these babies dying from something we had a cure for? I immediately began writing a proposal, requesting funds to travel to Nairobi, Kenya, to do volunteer work in community health, immunizing babies. I thought I would go over there and save those children.

The National Medical Fellowship funded the proposal, and I was able to work from Kenyatta National Hospital as a volunteer "foot doctor." We were called foot doctors because we walked from home to home throughout the hillside. I was part of a community medical team that went into the hillside villages of the Lake

Victoria area. I will never forget the seventeen-hour flight to Nairobi. I had one stopover in Frankfurt, Germany, where I tried to telephone a cousin who was stationed just outside of Frankfurt in a small city called Mainz, Germany. The instructions on use of the telephones at the airport were written in German, and the operator spoke only German, so it was difficult for me to reach my cousin. Every time I tried to ask a passerby for help, they looked at me in a condescending fashion and kept walking. Finally, my cousin telephoned me to see if I had arrived and came to airport to pick me up. I was able to stay overnight with them before departing for Nairobi the next day.

In Nairobi, people speak thirty-three different dialects, and although Swahili is the national language, most people speak their tribal dialect, and often they cannot understand each other. I could not understand anyone if they did not speak English because all I had was my Swahili dictionary, which I had studied briefly before I left the United States. Unfortunately, this dictionary did not have any of the dialects. As I later found out, many of those languages have never been written.

I telephoned Jean, the person the university had instructed me to contact upon arrival. Jean was British, and she rode a motorcycle. Luckily, I had traveled light. It was the first time I was ever on a motorbike. I stayed with Jean my first night in Nairobi. I remember it was extremely hot and the mosquitos were everywhere. My bed was surrounded by a mosquito net, but I was still frightened most of the night because I had read about malaria. The mosquitos were also much larger than the mosquitos in the United States. They were loud, so you could hear when they were surrounding you. They were less bothersome in the daytime.

The next morning, I got onto Jean's motorbike again and headed to Kenyatta, the national hospital, where I met the director of the community medicine program and was assigned to a team member. The person assigned to me was a tall, thin man with jet-black skin and hair. The deep black of his skin was a color I had never seen in America. He spoke several of the native dialects, and that was why I was assigned to him. Each day, we walked though the hillsides around Lake Victoria. The homes were made of mud and had thatched roofs. We entered home after home, and there was a level of poverty there I had never experienced. Some days, we had classes most of the day and did not go into the countryside. This is when I met with medical students who were curious about what it was like to live in America. Stella, one of the medical students, invited me to stay at her home in Kisumu, a city not far from Nairobi.

Stella's mom, a tall, elderly, Black woman with a medium build and hair as white as snow, picked me up in front of Kenyatta National Hospital in her black Rolls-Royce. We drove until we reached the countryside where her home sat on top of a hilltop. I asked Stella's mom where the boundaries to her land were. She explained that she owned thousands of acres and her land extended, she said, "as far as the eye can see." Thirty acres were devoted to citrus fruits that included oranges, and there was a dairy with cows. This was a different kind of farm than the one I grew up on. This was the first time I was not subjected to racism or discrimination. I was not aware of the stressful effects of racism until I visited this country and was completely removed, from it. The feeling is what one feels when a major burden has been removed or a serious problem has been solved. You sigh with relief.

I was escorted to my room and assigned a houseboy. The houseboy was an older black man who had worked for Stella's family for years. His job was to take care of me. He did my laundry, ran warm baths in the evening, prepared my breakfast, washed my clothing, and ironed. He was shorter than me, very petite, with shiny, deeply tanned, bronze-colored skin. He had a warm smile, bright white teeth, and a short afro. I enjoyed conversations with him at the end of the day; he always had questions about living in America. In the mornings, he would squeeze fresh orange juice from oranges grown in their orchard. He also placed lavender leaves from a tree inside a white handkerchief on my nightstand so that when I awoke, I would smell the sweet fragrance of lavender.

Stella's mom drove me back to the hospital each morning to meet the other members of my team, and then she would pick me up in the evening. Stella told me many of the people who worked for her mom also stole from her, so I asked Stella's mom about this one day. She said she did not care how much they stole from her and it was okay because they were just trying to feed and clothe their families. Her compassion was refreshing.

The people in Nairobi did not have the amenities we have in America. They would travel for miles in goat-pulled carts with a variety of medical conditions to get to our community clinic. I saw many infectious diseases that I had only read about in the United States. The dilemma I had to cope with was seeing the worst poverty imaginable during the day and then experiencing the comforts of extreme wealth in the evenings.

As a foot doctor, I traveled throughout the countryside on foot, even up into the mountains, where the women and men often smoked opium. Culturally, smoking opium was like smoking cigarettes in the United States. You could tell they smoked because when they smiled, you could see their black teeth. Opium has a very sweet smell, and my frequent encounters with the smoke had a euphoric effect on me. Sometimes, I realized that I was smiling for no reason.

Overall, Kenya was a wonderful experience. The people showed sincere gratitude for the help and care our team gave them, which reinforced my resolve to be a doctor. Over the years, I have stayed in touch with some of the friends I met there. For example, Stella worked for the Bill and Melinda Gates Foundation as a program officer for the infant AIDS program in Nairobi. I went back to Nairobi and took my family in early 2000, and my daughter and Stella met for the first time. What we did not know at that time was my daughter would be volunteering in Malawi and Cape Town, South Africa, as a dental student years later. As part of her preparation, she telephoned Stella, who now lives near Washington, DC, for information and contacts in Malawi. My volunteer experience in Kenya was memorable and was the start of many friendships.

There is a saying that "one true friend is greater than a thousand enemies," and my friendship with Stella has been lifelong.

CHAPTER 11

I MADE IT—THE MATCH

Don't try to learn everything on your own.
Every dream requires a team!

In the last year of medical school, I participated in what was called "the match." Each medical student is matched with a hospital for an internship and residency based on his or her choice of their specialty. I had always wanted to be a pediatrician, and I received honors in pediatrics. However, at the last minute, I decided to go into internal medicine because I felt it offered more options. I matched with the Columbia University College of Physicians and Surgeons and was assigned to work in one of their affiliates, Harlem Hospital, in New York City.

After four long years, I graduated from medical school. What a joyous day! It had not been a nurturing environment, but I had made it. All the minority students took photos together, and I still have this photograph in my office. Two of the three black students specialized in Dermatology, and I selected Internal Medicine. Having survived four years of medical school, I felt I could now survive just about anything that life might present to me.

An important note for prospective medical students is to select a medical school in a city or state where you would consider living. For example, if you know that you hate cold weather, apply to schools in milder climates. Also, it is wise to stay in one residency program and not relocate before completion. The contacts you make during medical school and residency are important when you enter the workforce. Often, these relationships determine what opportunities are available to you. I did not have this insight, but if I had, my career options may have been better.

CHAPTER 12

SILENT TEARS INTERNSHIP/ RESIDENCY

Success requires TEARS: Tenacity, Endurance, Authenticity, Resilience, and Soul!

The first year that you work in a hospital after getting your medical degree is called an "internship." Mine was literally the worst year of my life. The best thing about my internship was that it ended. But two more awful years followed. I felt a strange sense of accomplishment just because I had survived, although I don't know how I did it.

The first day of my internship, I arrived at the hospital at six in the morning. I was assigned a list of ten or twelve patients I was responsible for. This was a stressful time because I had never had this level of responsibility when taking care of patients. Standard practice is to assign an intern to a resident who is there to train, guide, and advise the intern. The residents that I had were very good in terms of answering questions and explaining things—when I could find them. Most of the time, however, I was on my own.

Fortunately, people on the nursing staff often had twenty to thirty years of experience, and they taught me about 60 percent of everything that I learned as a doctor. The nurses were like family and genuinely wanted me to succeed to be the best doctor I could be. I would not have survived my internship if it had not been for their constant encouragement and support.

As a first-year intern, my greatest fear was harming a patient. I did not want any of my patients to suffer because of my lack of knowledge and inexperience. This meant that despite working twelve-to-fourteen-hour days, I always had to make time to read.

Every third night, we were on call, which meant working continuously for twenty-four hours. When you were on call, there was usually little or no time for rest, sleep, or eating. I always tried to get a little sleep between ten o'clock and midnight. Then, I would get up and follow up on laboratory results and reevaluate each patient I had admitted. Usually at about two in the morning, I would begin writing notes for the day. We were required to write problem-oriented daily notes for each patient. Writing notes helped me organize my thoughts before presenting each case for morning rounds with the attending physician. Even though I was off duty the day after being on call, I still worked half the day, finishing up things I hadn't been able to complete during the night.

During my first year as an intern, I was paid about $16,000.00 even though I worked over sixty hours a week. This was barely enough to pay my rent in New York. There was no money to purchase a car, to travel, or to invest. I lived month to month and check to check. My financial situation was further exacerbated by all my school loans, which had become due the day I graduated. My mailbox was filled with notices from lenders informing me of loan repayment amounts. The financial burden continued for the next twenty years.

I had a wonderful attending physician during my intensive care unit (ICU) rotation. He had been an internist for many years and was extremely knowledgeable. The work was laborious, but his support, encouragement, and constant tutelage made it rewarding. Although he was in private practice, he still came to the hospital daily to make himself available and answer questions. Nevertheless, I had so many emotional scars at the end of internship that I never even considered doing a fellowship in a specialty because fellows were often treated like interns. I vowed to never be an intern again.

My internship year was followed by the first year of a three-year residency. Residency was a tremendous change in my life. The greatest responsibility in residency is teaching interns and trying hard to make sure they don't harm anyone. I was still doing a significant amount of direct patient care, but it was not as hard or as intimidating as during my internship. There was also more time to read. However, the thing that no one tells you is that you are in self-teaching mode to a large extent because the attending assigned to you is often not around. I was fortunate in my residency because at least one of the senior residents could usually be found somewhere in the hospital.

Residency had some definite perks. Some of my colleagues became lifelong friends; we've remained close even though we live in other states. My best friend and I interned together. I owe surviving my internship to her. She always supported me, and I could go to her for answers. We also helped each other with patient management when we could not find a senior resident or attending. As I've mentioned, one of the lessons I learned from my internship was that I could also learn a lot from the nurses, so for those readers who may have a medical internship, remember that it is important to establish good relationships with the nurses because they can teach you so much.

I relocated to California and completed my second year of residency at Los Angeles County University of Southern California (LAC+USC) Medical Center. Life at USC brought me into contact with two very different doctors. The first criticized and berated me on rounds with patients, medical students, and other residents. His behavior did not foster constructive learning, but there was no one else to turn to for help. The program director and administration already knew about this and chose to ignore it. Consequently, I learned to be silent and listen, never saying anything back.

What helped me survive during this time was positioning myself at the very back of the group, trying to put as much room between me and the attending as possible. This didn't always work. The color of my skin made it impossible for me to hide from him. I stood silently, asked no questions, and did not volunteer an answer even when I knew it. Again, my mother was there to encourage and help me survive.

I learned that, as a Black physician and as a woman, I would have to make certain concessions to survive. Life at USC was also a culture shock for me in other ways. I'd had several Black attending physicians in New York, but there was only one on staff at USC. He was a cardiologist. He had done research in cardiology for many years and was well respected in the medical community. Once I discovered that he was there, I signed up for the cardiology rotation. I enjoyed the rotation because he spent a great deal of time with the students on rounds and his bedside manner was exemplary. He never talked down to patients; he greeted them by name and introduced the students by name as well. On rounds, he would ask a patient's permission to demonstrate a specific finding. He listened and answered questions. His kindness and compassion were obvious to both patients and students. Best of all, he did not berate or harass me on a daily basis. But despite his kindness, I could not wait for the program to end. I was so relieved when I graduated and did not consider attending the ceremony. I received my certificate in the mail.

CHAPTER 13

GETTING HIRED— GIVE ME A BREAK

Who you know and who knows you is more important than what you know. A good education is not enough!

I was certain that I had done everything necessary to ensure a life of success as a physician. Following the completion of my internship and residency training in Internal Medicine, I started sending out my résumé. I was interviewed for several full-time positions. However, despite impeccable academic credentials, I found myself unable to land a job.

There are two positions in any situation: insiders and outsiders. People will always prefer those they already know, like and trust.

It soon became clear that all my years of education had failed me as a Black physician. I was told as much by my first interviewer who said, "They made me promise never to hire a Black person." The interview was with a major oil company in Los Angeles, California. It was for a staff physician position in their employee health clinic. The interviewer's office was small, and there was a window behind his desk that had a spectacular view of the tall buildings in downtown L.A. He was an elderly Caucasian gentleman, probably about sixty-five years of age, with white hair and blue eyes. He had a very tense but distinguished demeanor. He had assumed I was a man because there was no first name on my résumé. I had learned early to exclude my first name because women were sometimes excluded from interviews.

This interviewer had obviously expected someone other than a Black female physician and could not hide his shock when I walked in. His discomfort was obvious. The look on his face was that of a person straining to have a bowel movement. He had great difficulty getting the interview started, and even greater difficulty trying to find the right words to express his surprise. He knew it was a total waste of time to even act as if he would consider me. Then, he blurted out that the executives who had hired him had, about twenty years earlier, made him promise that he would never hire a Black person. He also indicated that he was Jewish and had attended a Jewish university in New York, as if that justified his choice.

He was visibly shaken, and I think he felt relieved that he had at least told the truth. He was very apologetic and kept telling me that it was his predecessor's decision, not his, and that it was beyond his control. That ended the interview. I left feeling humiliated. If I had known then what I know now, I would have considered filing a lawsuit against the company for discriminatory hiring practices. The interviews that followed also resulted in no job offers. The reality was that, at some point in my career, I was going to need to make it on my own. Furthermore, I had to be determined to succeed against all odds.

Finally, I took a part-time position outside my specialty in a feeble attempt to make ends meet and repay medical school debts. It was a temporary position that involved treating Intensive Care Unit (ICU) patients at California Hospital Medical Center in downtown Los Angeles. None of the physicians in the medical group wanted to take hospital night calls at the time. The company never offered me a full-time position, and the one black, male physician that they did hire years later had problems working for them.

Here I was, with a high school diploma, an additional eleven years of education—four years getting my bachelor's degree, four years of medical school for a doctorate, three years of internship and residency training—and I could not get a full-time job. I was barely able to support myself. My salary didn't quite cover the costs of renting an apartment, owning a car, and paying back my school loans. I was constantly juggling my finances to survive. More than once, I had to borrow money from my mother just to buy groceries. If you are thinking that there is something wrong with this picture, then you're right.

In a last-ditch effort to ward off starvation, I took a full-time job practicing occupational medicine with a government agency. Occupational medicine involves treating employees at a company-provided medical unit on a work site. Most of my time was spent treating work-related conditions, although some non-work-related services were also provided. In addition, I provided support on medical issues to non-medical departments, such as human resources, as well as ensuring the employer was in compliance with several federal regulations, such as the Americans with Disabilities Act (ADA) and so on.

This job was not easy to come by for a Black female physician. My three predecessors had been white male physicians, and I was only offered the position once each of them had resigned.

GETTING HIRED—GIVE ME A BREAK

In this position, I was asked questions regarding employees' potential toxic exposure. For example, I was asked if there were any potential adverse health effects with regard to an employee who had been exposed to thalidomide. The thalidomide was inside a test tube that had broken in transport. After extensive research and tracking the source of this substance, which was being sent for research purposes, I was able to answer the question. This situation and several others that followed made me acutely aware that I needed knowledge and training in the field of toxicology, training I did not get in medical school. So I started taking classes in toxicology at the UCLA School of Public Health. I also asked my boss if I could be reimbursed for the classes, which were quite costly. After he said yes, I decided to enroll in classes that would result in the completion of the master's degree in public health with an emphasis in toxicology. The toxicology courses helped me fill a gap in knowledge that I needed for work. But, it was difficult trying to work full-time and take classes at night. Also, don't forget I was still financially stressed by my school loans.

After I had worked for this company about two years, they started hiring new doctors and paying them $10,000 more per year than I was earning after working there for two years. I asked my boss about this, and he reminded me that I was the only one who had signed the contract agreeing to the salary offered. He said, "No one made you take it." This was the ultimate humiliation, so I decided to resign.

It was during this experience that I realized that you really don't do your best work when you have been discriminated against. It makes you feel violated. I thought it was best for me to leave. My boss agreed to have me remain as a contractor, but few clients were referred to me. I learned from this experience that a signed contract does not ensure that the other party will use your services.

Years later, I negotiated a contract to provide services on-site and part-time as an associate medical director. With this contract, I could reap the financial rewards I had not obtained previously.

Sexual harassment was the other reason I left this position. I either had to leave or file a lawsuit against them. I strongly considered the lawsuit, but I knew they would retaliate and get rid of me anyway. I received daily telephone calls from about fifty women whom I had never met requesting that I include their names on a class-action lawsuit for sexual harassment against the supervisor I considered suing. Ultimately, I decided to leave the organization on the best terms possible.

If you're a woman, you will encounter sexual harassment, especially in professional fields. Consider getting counseling early in your career to prepare you for the best way to handle it.

CHAPTER 14

PRIVATE PRACTICE – NAVIGATION WITH NO MAP

You need at least three profit centers in your career orbusiness that are independent of one another.

Not being successful in the job market, I decided to open my own private practice in internal medicine. Then, I realized, there was absolutely no discussion about private practice in medical school. We received no training or education on what was required to open one's own office. I did not have any physicians in my family who could advise me during this process, so I had no idea where to start or what I was doing. In addition, college had not taught me any entrepreneurial skills.

Nevertheless, common sense told me I needed to secure financing. I asked a local bank what I had to do to get start-up money. I was told that I needed a business plan, among other things. I immediately started working on it. I based it on the realities of private practice. For example, I showed little or no projected income for the first three months. The first nine banks that I approached turned me down. They were not loaning money to new businesses at that time.

PRIVATE PRACTICE — NAVIGATION WITH NO MAP

Finally, I met a Black woman working at one of the banks who explained that the business had to show a profit from day one. I went back and fixed my business plan, making my business look better on paper. I said I would see a lot of patients the first month and the numbers would continue to grow. I would be making a lot of money, at least on paper. But even with these revisions, the next bank turned me down. I was turned down by the next eight banks.

I decided to go back and ask one of the banks what was wrong with my business plan. An officer sat down with me and made some suggestions. Again, I revised the plan and submitted it to another bank. I was still not able to secure any funding.

There was a foreign bank in downtown Los Angeles. Since all of the American banks had turned me down, I decided to try it. I went in with my business plan, and they approved my start-up loan request. I was elated that now I could begin looking for office space and start my own practice. The loan terms were tough. They charged three times the interest of other banks, and they required a disability policy as security for the loan that cost me $3,000.00 per quarter.

I learned many important lessons in this transaction. First, do not try to do everything on my own. Get help from business professionals.

It's also important to ask for enough capital to succeed. Many small-business owners make the mistake of not asking for enough money up front, resulting in financial difficulties later. I asked for $150,000.00 and I got it. I was able to pay the bank back earlier than scheduled as well as run my business for the first year without having to worry about finances.

There was also a class at UCLA on starting a business that I enrolled in. It provided general information needed for start-ups. I learned about accounting, bookkeeping, staffing, and more. The class didn't focus on medical practices, but it was better than nothing.

I opened the doors to my practice on April 25, 1985, in Culver City, California. I'll never forget the first day in my office. I had a patient walk in, a middle-aged woman who was very sick. I had to help her onto the examination table. I worked to stabilize her for over an hour in my office before transferring her to the hospital. We sent her bill to Medi-Cal, and they sent me a check for eighty-nine cents. I framed it and hung it on the wall in my office, partly to celebrate my accomplishment and partly to remind myself what accepting Medi-Cal insurance would get me.

Dealing with insurance was a major eye-opening experience for me. I wanted to help underserved patients, but I had to make enough money to keep my office open. It took approximately two years for me to build a substantial private practice that I could easily pay my monthly bills with. I was fortunate that several subspecialists in my office building referred patients to me. There was a gynecologist who referred all of his patients with internal medicine problems to me. Across the hallway from my office was an orthopedic surgeon who allowed me to do many of his preoperative medical evaluations. This, along with being on the emergency-room call panels at several local hospitals, helped tremendously. It was not long before I was treating ten to fourteen patients per day in the office, sometimes six or eight patients in the hospital and four in the ICU. Despite all of this, for the next ten years, I struggled to repay my medical school loans.

I also asked my husband to share my office. We did some minor construction that was costly but helped to consolidate our business expenses. I was able to survive, but I still needed to generate other income to repay my loans. I had to become creative to make a living in medicine. I could not just sit in my office and wait for patients to walk in.

I became a physician entrepreneur and started marketing my practice. This resulted in securing a contract as a drug-testing site for a major employer. This helped in two ways because sometimes those clients would become patients in my office.

Cash flow can be a big challenge for small-business owners and self-employed professionals. You can have three great months and two terrible ones. You must learn to use your creativity to create multiple streams of income.

In terms of staffing, I was able to hire an office manager who was also an accountant, and her experience was a tremendous help to me. Necessity became the mother of invention. Hiring medical staff that were still in training and providing on-site training for them helped cut costs. This also allowed me to hire them once their training ended. This was especially good for the back-office position, because this person worked directly under my supervision.

The front-office position required an experienced and compassionate person. Your front-office staff is critical for a new office. Fortunately, my secretary was excellent, and she was with me for many years. She was smart, patient, and dependable. Hire the best people you can, and pay them well.

I also sought out other physicians and business owners. I asked one doctor how he handled his medical billing. He told me that he had gone over to the hospital and offered someone who was working in their billing department more money and better benefits.

Location is also important. I opened my practice in a medical complex across the street from a major hospital. I was on staff at that hospital and at two others in downtown Los Angeles, about forty-five minutes away.

PRIVATE PRACTICE — NAVIGATION WITH NO MAP

This made it easy to do hospital rounds on my patients who required hospitalization.

Private practice was wonderful, and I really enjoyed developing relationships with my patients. Many of them were like family. Regrettably, I also learned that some Black patients don't like going to Black physicians. They felt they were not getting the best care unless the doctor was Caucasian. This was so shocking to me that I discussed it with an older, Black physician who had been practicing for many years. His response was, "Well, nothing has changed."

In my private practice, 60 percent of the patients were Caucasian, 30 percent were Hispanic, and about 10 percent were Black. Many of my patients were professional women and senior citizens.

I had been in practice for about five years before health-maintenance organizations (HMOs) were taking over much of the primary care market. It became very difficult for the solo practitioner to compete with them. I lost a substantial part of my practice because the HMOs would actually knock on the doors of senior citizen and sign them up. These patients didn't know what they were being switched to. Patients would come in and we would send the bill to the insurance company or Medicare, and it would be returned unpaid. That's when the patients and our office realized the HMOs had gotten them signed up.

It didn't take long for me to see the writing on the wall. It's important to understand the trends in your industry. Ask yourself, If things continue as they are, what is likely to be true ten years from now? Then, look for ways to position yourself to take full advantage of where things are going. Don't put all of your eggs in one basket. You need at least three profit centers at all times. This is a very important lesson, regardless of your career, business, or profession.

It's also important to continue developing new relationships and income streams, no matter how successful you become.

CHAPTER 15

THE "ISMS" CAN'T STOP ME—RACISM AND SEXISM

The ugly truth is that you may encounter racism and sexism if you are a woman of color. Both are alive and well.

I continued my full-time clinical practice for about ten years as well as working in occupational medicine. Intermittently, I would apply for positions that I thought were interesting. For example, I applied for a position with the Veterans Administration (VA). There were three vacant staff positions. I interviewed for all three positions and was not selected for any of them. The interview with the chief of the department—the one you may think would have carried the most weight—took less than ten minutes. He said two things to me: "Tell me something about yourself," and, "Can you type?" I recall thinking, does he think I'm interviewing to be his secretary? I really wasn't sure. It was clear from the interview that he had no genuine intention of considering me for any position. A few days later, I received a letter stating that more qualified applicants had been selected.

Ultimately, they filled two positions with people who had completed their residency training programs

THE "ISMS" CAN'T STOP ME—RACISM AND SEXISM

with the VA, and the other was a doctor who was already working for the VA. I question whether these were more qualified applicants, considering, at that point, I had a master's degree, had completed an internship and a residency, and was board certified. The VA had more than two hundred physicians that year, only two of them were black. Their discriminatory hiring practices continue to this day.

In the early part of 2002, I applied for a health-care-leadership fellowship and was accepted. One of the doctors in charge of the program had retired from a large, private insurance company the year before, and his position was being advertised in medical journals. I applied for the position and asked if he would assist me in getting an interview. He let me know that he had left the company a year earlier and he'd had no contact with it since. Therefore, he was not in a position to assist me. He also said that he had nothing to do with their selection process.

None of what he said to me was truthful, but I accepted his explanation.

Approximately four months later, I was sitting in a continuing education class in San Diego with nearly four hundred other physicians. I decided to chat with a white, male doctor sitting next to me that I will refer to as Ted. I asked Ted, "What brings you to this conference?" He explained that he was the medical director of a large insurance company. I asked, "What insurance company?" It happened to be the same company that the head of the leadership fellowship had retired from. I thought what a coincidence. In this room of over four hundred doctors, as fate would have it, I sat next to Ted. Then I asked, "How did you get the position?"

He responded, "What happened was someone I know," then he mentioned the previous medical director's name, "called me one day and asked if I wanted

THE "ISMS" CAN'T STOP ME—RACISM AND SEXISM

his position because he was going to retire. I said yes." What was clear to me was the "old boy network" was still alive and well. Ted was basically selected for the job before it was even advertised. So even though this position had been advertised and applicants would be interviewed, Ted had already been selected for the position.

I said, "Oh, I see. What kind of salary do you get in that kind of position—just the range?" He let me know that he was well compensated with about $300,000 per year. He explained that to maintain his position, he needed to become board certified in internal medicine and that this was why he was taking the class we were in. There I was, board certified for years and taking the course for recertification, yet the insurance company had not even considered me for an interview. Yes, the good ol' boy network was alive and well.

Another interesting experience was when I interviewed for a position with a government agency that performed audits of medical facilities in Los Angeles County. I had come across the advertisement on the Internet. The interviewer indicated that he was hiring for two positions—one in Orange County and one in San Bernardino County. The one in San Bernardino County was closer to me, so I told him that was the one I was most interested in.

Three weeks later, I had heard nothing. I called the interviewer's office. He returned my call, indicating that he was still considering me but none of my references had gotten back to him. I told him that I would follow up again in a couple of days. As soon as I got off the phone with him, I called the three physicians that I had provided as references. They all said that they hadn't received telephone calls or correspondence from the interviewer. When I followed up with him a couple of weeks later, he said he had already hired someone for the position in Orange County but would get back to me as soon as he finished processing my application and references. I did not tell him that I knew he had not contacted them. Then, I received an e-mail thanking me for interviewing but saying they were no longer hiring for the San Bernardino County.

Two months later, the position was again posted for both locations. I immediately called the contact and said that I had already submitted an application. Could I be considered? He explained that the doctor they had hired for Orange County did not work out and that he was not sure the San Bernardino position was going to be funded. About two weeks later, I called him again. This time, he told me that he had filled the Orange County position and was holding the San Bernardino position for me, trying to finalize the funding. One week later, I received a letter informing me that the San Bernardino position no longer existed. In my heart, I knew that I had never really been considered for either position.

Years later, I applied for a position with another government agency as a staff physician. During the interview, I was told that there were no positions available at any of their southern California facilities but that I could be considered for those in central California. Since I had not been interviewed for the southern California positions that I had applied for and they were still posted on the website as vacant, I reapplied. I was never able to get an interview. They hired four physicians in southern California who had applied after me for positions that they had told me did not exist. None of the selectees were black and one of them had not even completed his residency at the time he was hired.

Yes, discrimination and racism are alive and well in America. This is when you realize that the early years of a child's life are so important. How fortunate and grateful I am that two loving, remarkable, resilient, joyful

THE "ISMS" CAN'T STOP ME—RACISM AND SEXISM

people—pillars of faith, strength, and understanding—were at the center of the first five years of my life. I cannot know how much of my character and endurance was molded by their relentless lessons and belief in me, but it was considerable.

While in private practice, I had also applied for government contracts that had a minority, small-business, and/or woman-owned-business minority set-aside. After their selections had been made, I called to find out why a minority applicant had not been selected. I was told that set-asides were only goals and that sometimes the agencies didn't meet their goals. In other words, there was no requirement to select minorities, women, or small-business owners. It became clear that minority set-asides on government contracts were in my opinion to ensure that there was no participation of Black Americans.

Through the years, I have continued to send out applications and résumés intermittently, whenever I've found a position that I might like in Internal Medicine. I've had some wonderful interviews for interesting positions. My experience is that government positions are often filled before interviews, which are just a formality. They can say they interviewed everyone who applied even though they already knew whom they were going to hire. Similarly, in the corporate setting, selection is based on who you know. The bottom line is that it's not *what* you know; it's also important who you know and who knows you. You must be ready to switch careers if you need to.

There is still a lack of diversity in US health care. Specifically, there has been no significant increase in the percentage of Black American physicians who were descendants of slaves in the past one hundred years. During the four years I was a medical student, I never saw a black instructor from any country. I do not know what the status is at other medical schools except the

THE "ISMS" CAN'T STOP ME—RACISM AND SEXISM

historically black universities. It is common practice to admit to medical schools and/or hire Black persons from Africa and India who may have a black skin color but who are not descendants of Black American slaves and who may not even be US citizens.

CHAPTER 16

PHYSICIAN ENTREPRENEUR

Look for opportunities outside of your specialty, where your skills are transferable.

The ugly truth is that you may encounter racism and sexism, especially if you are a woman of color; both are alive and well in America.

Furthermore, despite what most people would consider "great progress" over the last half century, the percentage of Black physicians in the United States who are of descendants of slaves has actually decreased. The situation for women isn't much better. Women still earn less than their male counterparts in just about every profession. These statistics belie that old strategy of getting a good education and working for a solid company. Frankly, it has never worked very well for women or people of color.

The days when someone could simply get a college degree, enter into a management training program, and expect thirty to forty years of promotions and pay raises is over. No one has the luxury of depending on a benevolent employer to provide lifetime job security. That ship has sailed, even for the well-educated, white male. This book is a wake-up call, particularly for women and people of color. For too long, we've been setting our sights on an illusory goal. We thought that if we just studied hard enough and worked hard enough that we would be given our slices of the pie. Well, I'm here to tell you that the pie is no longer offered up on a platter. If you want a slice, you're going to have to go out and bake your own pie. That's exactly what I've had to do over the last three decades. I've had to slowly forget the notion that someone was going to reward all my years of study with a dream job. I was the one who was dreaming, and I needed to wake up. In many fields, the best jobs are not available to women and people of color, regardless of our qualifications.

I've had to hustle to make a living in medicine. There were no other choices. Changing careers was not an option because I had invested in four years of college, four years of medical school, one year of internship, two years of residency, and five years obtaining a master's degree in public health. I also had $300,000.00 of student debt. I should have been able to make a decent living, having made this kind of investment.

Unstoppable is what I had to be if I wanted to succeed. I had to learn to use rejection from others as fuel to help me move on to the next challenge. There were times when I just prayed to make it to the next day, and when it became hard, I tried to just make it to the next moment. I would reflect on the journey of my ancestors and slavery, and somehow, deep in the depths of my soul, I would find the strength to carry on.

I realize that there are many professionals out there not only in health care but in other fields who may have had similar experiences. We grew up in households where our parents told us that if we just got an education, we would be okay and not have the same struggles and difficult lives they had. I was encouraged to get the best education possible to ensure a better life for myself. In many ways, that did not work out for me, and it probably has not for some others as well. This old-fashioned thinking has paralyzed people. You've likely read newspaper stories about well-educated people being unemployed for years or reports of thousands of new college graduates working in minimum-wage jobs outside their intended professions.

To succeed today, you must learn to think and act differently. You cannot rely on getting a job in your chosen field or having a job for life.

You must use your knowledge and skills to find or create new opportunities for yourself. You must learn to become entrepreneurial in your approach. That's what I had to do. I hope that this book serves as a wake-up call for young people.

Formal education isn't enough. While studying to be a doctor, a lawyer, an engineer, or whatever else you choose, it is also important to study to become an entrepreneur. This is not taught in most professional schools. You're going to have to learn it on your own. This means taking business courses as well as courses in your chosen career field. It also means laying the foundation for a future business by making the right connections, building the proper credit profile, and so on.

I realize that this must sound strange coming from a physician. You don't typically think of doctors as entrepreneurs. You may not have ever have thought of yourself as an entrepreneur. Let this book teach you that you must be able to reinvent yourself at some point, professionally and as an entrepreneur. You may have a dream job today, but there is no guarantee that you will have it tomorrow. Things change, and they seem to be changing faster all the time. You must be prepared for the next wave of change in your industry and have a plan to jump ship if the current gets too strong. Being an entrepreneurial professional is your best bet.

Flexibility, the ability to go with the flow and mold my skills into those needed in other areas, has been key to my success. For example, I did not plan to go into occupational medicine, but after doing so, I used the expertise to create a lucrative consulting business. That's flexibility.

Thinking creatively allowed me to work in the ICU at a California hospital and admit patients to a private hospital for chemically dependent patients.

Because of my training in toxicology, I was able to do toxicology consults. For example, I evaluated migrant workers exposed to toxins in the fields and was able to answer questions with regard to the Alaskan pipeline, as well as on other toxicology consults.

The skills I obtained working for a government agency in workers' compensation was leveraged to start my own worker's compensation consulting business. I had to put my entrepreneurial hat on and market that business. Several companies allowed me to review complex workers' compensation cases and make medical recommendations for cost containment. I was also able to secure a contract with a large insurance firm to review files in liability cases when injuries involved were in Internal Medicine.

I also applied for admitting privileges at a local community hospital for patients who had chemical dependencies and drug addictions. Once this was approved, I was referred patients whom I had admitted to the hospital upon their discharge.

The loss of patients in my private practice to Health Maintenance Organizations (HMOs) also forced me to become more entrepreneurial. I've mentioned earlier that the location of your office is important. My office was located one block from MGM Studios, so I would respond to calls from the studio. Remember the movie

Rocky? I treated one of the actors, who became ill on set. It was not only an enjoyable experience, but it was also lucrative, as I was paid well for my services. These kinds of opportunities enabled me to keep my office open. Ultimately, all of these things combined helped me to keep going financially for years.

You must develop a skill set that allows you to think "inside the box, outside the box, and when there is no box," as quoted on New York University's School of Business's website. I did this for years because of need and could probably teach a course on how this works in the real world.

My sincere hope is that you won't have to endure the obstacles that I have encountered. But either way, it's important to prepare yourself to be an entrepreneurial professional.

I'm not knocking the concept of higher education. It's important to obtain the best education and training available. I wouldn't trade my formal education for anything. I rely on my knowledge every day to make a living. I simply want to point out that education and training may not be enough to compete effectively in our new economy.

Success today requires more than technical or professional proficiency. You need to develop an entrepreneurial mind-set. You need the ability to thrive professionally without a job. You need to be able to create your own career, because, believe me, no one is going to do it for you.

I thought my master's degree in public health (MPH) might ultimately advance my career and allow me to transition into the field of public health. So I started searching for and applying for public health positions. It was not long before I discovered there were even fewer job opportunities in this field. I was never selected for any of the positions I applied for. It was always the white doctor that was selected, so that road was a dead end.

In hindsight, I would recommend you investigate job opportunities in a specific field before you engage time and money obtaining a degree. In addition, all of your college and graduate course work should be completed while you are still young. It is too hard to be a full-time student once you have all the responsibilities of a job and family. It was difficult for me to go back to school and work on the master's degree because I was a mother and wife, and was in the process of transitioning into a new clinical practice in Internal Medicine. But continuing your professional growth and development is essential for success.

The half-life of a medical education has been estimated to be four years. That means at that point, half of what a doctor learned in medical school is outdated. There are new discoveries being made all the time. I believe the same is true of most professions. You don't need to enroll in a degree program to continue your professional development. Enroll in seminars, take classes, and continually look for ways to improve your skills. This will not only help you become more confident professionally, but it will also help you keep growing as a person.

CHAPTER 17

MASTER SKILLS FOR PROFESSIONAL SUCCESS

The only thing that will never die is the "old boy," system.

In September of 2011, I was the associate medical director for a large government agency on a part-time basis. This was the same agency I had worked for previously and resigned from due to sexual harassment and being underpaid.

Nevertheless, in this role, I was intimately involved with employees threatened by exposure to anthrax in the mail. As a physician consultant and toxicologist, I was questioned on several occasions with regard to these potential exposures.

Suddenly, I was being summoned to the workroom floor because an unidentified white powder had been found. Even baby powder was presumed to be anthrax. I quickly had to become an expert on anthrax. The Center for Disease Control (CDC) had designed guidelines for how to handle potential exposures that I had to ensure were implemented. This included contacting the hazardous materials team that at work was referred to as "HAZMAT."

When the team arrived, they would be clothed in special protective clothing that included wearing special respirators. I felt as if I were suddenly on another planet, watching all of it as a spectator. But I was not a spectator, and when the decontamination process began, I was intimately involved. There were stations set up for all potentially exposed employees to be decontaminated, which consisted of being hosed down with cold water. This was not something you really wanted to be engaged in at work, but it was necessary to follow protocol. None of the facilities that were under my jurisdiction were ever exposed to anthrax.

Ultimately, this agency sustained substantial financial losses related to this bioterrorist act and did not renew any of the physician consultant contracts the following year.

Anticipate change. There are seasons and cycles in every career, business and profession.

Fortunately, my private practice was still going, but the end of that position was a substantial loss of income, and I returned to the job market. It quickly became obvious that even though more years had passed it was difficult to get interviews for positions and even harder to get selected for a position. Sadly, things were still the same in the job market in terms of white physicians having priority in hiring. What had changed was that the discriminatory hiring practices were more subtle, and more difficult to prove but still present.

Nevertheless, because of the free time that I had, I was able to volunteer time and money to help adolescents in the community with drug addictions. I wrote and implemented a program for adolescent drug users who were in foster care. This program helped approximately 350 children. I was also able to negotiate services for children in our program from a well-known chemical dependency rehabilitation provider in our city. The program continued for about five years.

I had embarked on a journey that ultimately led to success in my chosen field. Along this path, I have owned and operated a medical practice, a consulting firm, and a nonprofit agency. I have worked and consulted for government agencies and some of the largest insurance companies in the country. In short, I have learned not only to survive as a doctor but also to thrive as an entrepreneur. The more complicated my financial situation became, the more creative I had to become. My consulting business did so well that I eventually paid off all my school loans. This removed a tremendous monthly financial burden and improved the quality of my life; I could hire additional staff, work part-time in my clinical practice, and take more family vacations.

It was also during this time that I started making more real-estate investments. I would encourage anyone going into the medical profession (or any other profession) to consider investing early. If not for my real-estate investments, I would be having a much harder time right now. I am living proof that you can survive and thrive.

CHAPTER 18

REFLECTIVE LESSONS

"Success is not about the car you drive. It's about the place you're going. It's not about who you know. It's about who you are."

It took a lot of gumption and conviction for me to decide that I wanted to be a doctor in this country. There were many signs that suggested my goal was outrageous, considering I was a Black girl in America from the cotton fields and tobacco row of North Carolina, born to an impoverished, single, teenage mother before the Civil Rights Act. But I did not let being poor keep me from having dreams and going after them. In fact, I was poor the entire time I was a student. I believe this is where the term "poor student" comes from, but it is a temporary condition.

Although becoming a physician was more difficult than I could ever have imagined, the real lesson was who I had to become in the process. There are issues that I have walled off in my mind. For example, I still have a hard time dealing with death. I have had to block out big chunks of my life just so I could move on. I realize I have difficulty communicating in an emotional way.

REFLECTIVE LESSONS

Some of these things I did not realize until I started writing this book and was forced to revisit certain parts of my life. It's like a relationship gone bad after many years, where you love the person but you don't like what you have been through. So to deal with it you just don't talk about it. I have never been on a couch with a therapist, and maybe, in some small way, writing this book has been therapy.

Maybe my great-grandparents were trying to shelter me from demeaning experiences, like the one at the bus stop that I described in the earlier chapter called Just Raindrops. They wanted to protect me from the discrimination they experienced working on the farm, in the cotton fields, going into town to buy groceries, and of everyday life for them living in the South. They never talked about how they felt about these things in front of me, possibly because they did not want me to grow up hating anyone. If they were still here, I would tell them, don't suffer in silence. Open your mouth. Tell yourself you don't deserve this, and speak up!

They were probably fearful of repercussions if they voiced how they really felt and of what might have happened to me if I spoke out. I learned to stand tall and sometimes would tell myself, this too shall pass when things were difficult. I would ask God, if he were still listening to tell me what is all this about? It is time for me to be free from all of these things I don't want to talk about.

Nevertheless, there were some good experiences during my career journey that created lifelong memories. For example, I was able to climb Mount Kenya, when I was a volunteer "foot doctor." This allowed me to meet fellow mountain climbers from all over the world. In Egypt, I was able to spend time with a Nubian family, and visit the part of Egypt where the "garbage people" lived, cruise along the Nile River, and explore the

REFLECTIVE LESSONS

Pyramids of Giza. On the road to Mombasa, a small island along the east coast of Kenya, the tour bus stopped as giraffes crossed the road, a reminder that I was a long way from home.

I would advise you to try not to forget the things that you enjoy as you embark on your career. It is easy to put yourself last on the list of things to take care of because of the time commitment of any profession. It was difficult, but I had to remind myself that I loved to sing and at one time, I wanted to be a backup singer for Patti La Belle. Schedule time for yourself and the things you enjoy. I enjoyed international travel and meeting people from different cultures, so I planned vacations abroad about every two years. It also took that long to pay for them. Reconnect with and integrate the things that you enjoy into your life. You will be more successful and enjoy the journey if you can do this. Somehow, you have to treat yourself well, because others may not.

Throughout this book, there are some key lessons that I learned from my personal and professional journey. Some of them are outlined below:

1. Get the best education you can. Degrees and certifications do have value. They are needed to get in the door. The study and discipline required will also help you prepare for opportunities in the future.
2. Relationships are all that matter when it is all said and done.
3. Try not to forget the things that bring joy to your life and do at least one of those every day.
4. Significant success in any area of life requires mentorship. Mentorship is especially important to minority children. Be a mentor when you can.

5. Invest time shadowing and talking to people in the profession you think you want to be in.
6. Volunteer time with a nonprofit organization in your community. The rewards are great.
7. Take care of your grandparents. If you do not have grandparents, then help another elderly person in your community.
8. Do the research: talk to people, get on the Internet, and go to the library.
9. Learn to be a confident communicator. Join Toastmasters International to develop confidence in your public speaking.
10. Building a network of people to introduce you to others people and opportunities is essential for professional advancement.
11. Take a course in networking. Regularly attend networking events and conferences.

12. Read books like How to Win Friends & Influence People by Dale Carnegie. Investing time to build and strengthen relationships will pay off throughout your lifetime.
13. Prioritize and schedule time with your family. Your children need things that they can only get from you, and time is the one thing you cannot get back.
14. Take care of your health. Your health is more important than money. Don't work when you're sick, and exercise every day or at least three times a week.
15. You must learn to make your money work for you. Most people don't have rich parents or access to financial advisors. But you can educate yourself by reading and attending seminars on finance.

16. Pick at least one area to invest in. Learn what it takes to succeed in it, and get started as early as possible. I chose real estate investments.
17. Anticipate change. There are seasons and cycles in every career, business, and profession. Breakthroughs in understanding and new technologies bring accelerated change. Most people are overwhelmed by change. They have trouble adapting. The people who succeed in the long term anticipate change and welcome new discoveries.
18. Become politically savvy. Politics is simply the process of working in relationships and organizations to advance your goals. People call it politics, but what's really going on is insiders looking out for themselves and one another. This is always the reality.

My hope is that some of the above comments as well as the information provided in this book will assist you in your career endeavors and that you will be able to anticipate and/or avoid many of the challenges I encountered. Unfortunately, there are no second chances in life, but my hope is that you can learn something from the mistakes that I have made that will keep you from falling as many times as I did.

CHAPTER 19

CHANGING THE FACE OF MEDICINE

"Health Disparities," is the new euphemism for persistent racism in medicine.

The changes necessary in the field of medicine are systemic. There are no easy answers to the challenges we face now or in the future. Government is not necessarily the solution. But the federal government must be willing to do everything in its power to advance change where business and industries find it too costly or inconvenient. Here are just a few of the issues we must address:

1. Elimination of health disparities.

    There is still inequality in medicine. Giving everyone access to health care doesn't guarantee that everyone will receive the same quality of care. In our current health care system, the opposite is true. Underrepresented persons of color have greater morbidity and die at earlier ages from preventable medical conditions. My vision for health care is for every patient to receive the same quality of care, regardless of skin color and/or the language he or she speaks.

2. Community health care must become the best health care.

   We must explore new business and financial models for providing free or low-cost medical and dental services through community health clinics. Investing in preventative medicine can be more cost-effective long term.

3. The financial considerations of operating your own medical practice should be included in the medical curriculum.

   Financial mismanagement in health care is rampant. Teaching doctors about business finance might result in more efficient operation of medical practices and significant cost containment of health care dollars.

4. Incorporate medical practice development into medical schools' curricula.
5. Significantly increase the percentage of Black American doctoral students by developing scholarships based upon financial need that follow the student.

    No matter what institution a student selects, financial aid and/or scholarships that are based upon financial need and government funded should follow the student. This would help encourage and promote more diversity in the health care workforce.
6. Eliminate government-funded programs with goals and set-asides for minority participation that have excluded Black Americans of slave descent.
7. Eliminate MCAT scores for medical school (and dental school) because these tests exclude

many otherwise qualified students who want to be doctors and there is nothing being tested that is used in medical/dental school.

8. Black American students born in the United States and that are US citizens (and descendants of the slaves in this country) should have their tuition waived from college through a doctoral level of education, including medical/dental school. This would be in exchange for the four hundred years of free labor their ancestors contributed to the wealth of this country that has never been paid.

9. Tutors should be made available at all levels of education for Black American children born in this country who are descendants of slaves at no cost to the child.

10. Free health care should be provided to the poorest of the poor, Black American seniors that are descendants of slaves.

11. Equal opportunities should be created for Black Americans who are descendants of slavery. For example, it is common practice to send Black American men and women for leadership training and then deny them leadership opportunities. Another example is enrolling Black American children in science and pipeline programs and then denying them jobs in these professions after they earn degrees in these fields.

12. The American Medical Association (AMA) should legally support Black American physicians who are denied hospital privileges in this country. For example, I was denied hospital privileges at Eisenhower Hospital in Rancho Mirage, California, although I met all of their bylaw requirements.

13. Black American high school students need help completing the college admission process, so

there is a need for special counselors to assist them who are culturally competent and who genuinely care about their success.
14. Create government programs that result in increased participation and/or selection of Black Americans who are descendants of slaves who continue to encounter discrimination despite the Civil Rights Act.

I finally had to wake up to the realities of the health care system in America. Over thirty years of education and board certification in my specialty was not enough. I still encountered tremendous challenges trying to secure opportunities in medicine. This is obviously not progress and I question whether it represents equal opportunity.

Unfortunately, I learned many lessons the hard way. My sincere hope is that the reader will take courage from my story and realize that no matter the obstacles in your path, you can overcome them and achieve success.

CHAPTER 20

RECONCILIATION

Grandma said, "Everyone has a cross to bear."

The decision to become a doctor was the most challenging and the most rewarding of my life, but no one really talks about the racism, sexism, and discrimination in healthcare.

Perhaps no one discusses it because they feel comfort in believing that racism and sexism no longer exist—in medicine or in other professions. There can be shame and humiliation in knowing that you are an intelligent person who has spent years securing degrees, but you are still unemployable. I doubt if I was ever seriously considered for most of the positions I was clearly qualified for, and this was the result of a deep and serious problem in our society.

Despite the challenges, I ultimately realized that years of investing in myself qualified me to work for myself and be responsible for my own future.

My life has been an exercise in determination, but it is important for you to work toward the decision of whether you want to pursue a healthcare career yourself.

RECONCILIATION

You can either learn lessons the hard way or listen to someone who has been there and done it.

This book was a summary of some of my real-life experiences after choosing a career in medicine. My hope is that some of these experiences will inspire you.

ABOUT THE AUTHOR

VICKIE Y. MABRY-HEIGHT, M.D., M.P.H., F.A.C.P., "COL"

I am a board certified physician with more three decades of expertise and practice in the specialty of Internal Medicine.

As the first person in my family to go to college, it was a happy day when I graduated from York College of the City University of New York. This was followed by completion of a medical doctorate at Albert Einstein College of Medicine of Yeshiva University. My specialty training in Internal Medicine was obtained from Columbia College of Physicians & Surgeons. The senior residency in Internal Medicine was completed at the University of Southern California and Good Samaritan Hospital.

The Master's degree in Public Health (M.P.H.) with an emphasis in environmental & occupational toxicology was earned at U.C.L.A. I am a Fellow of the American College of Physicians (F.A.C.P.).-

For more information about me and my work, please visit my website at www.MabryHeightMD.com.

www.ingramcontent.com/pod-product-compliance
Lightning Source LLC
Chambersburg PA
CBHW060525100426
42743CB00009B/1435